My Initial Scribble Poesy

Creedance Grace

BookLeaf Publishing

Presentation by *BookLeaf Publishing*

Web: www.bookleafpub.com

E-mail: info@bookleafpub.com

ISBN: 9789357616058

First edition 2022

To my daughter

Bloom like poetry

It is the gift of spirit, the birth of life
The beginning of new, face East to rise
The blossom of Spring, create your own drum
Believe in your rhythm, your life has just began

You live and you grow, you learn from living
You rise with the Sun, its Summer in the South
You create your own wheel, in parts of four
Called the Circle Of Life, its meaning is so
much more

Mother Earth and all aspects of life;
Journey our own cycle, we all have our own
times
Nurture West of your emotions, fall in love with
yourself
Your life is so beautiful, look all around

The moon shines so bright, lighting the winter in
the North
Your tipi is complete now; you bathe in the life
you choose
The four aspects of the medicine wheel,
connects close to home

The Spiritual, Physical, Emotional and Mental
state,
is a powerful gift to behold

Elegy - Life Itself

Hard to speak on death, but easy to remember
who we lost;
Missing and Murdered Women, And all those
who are lost.

Canadian soil is where it takes place, across the
Country;
In every single 'Safe Place'.

We honor our Women, We honor our Men.
We honor those who are gone; the ones whom
left from wrong.

And we honor those who are alive, living drug
led lives.
God loves us all, he truly understands.

But why is there death and after-life;
when we were given only one chance at this life.

Cause the life we live in now seems so unfair;
I am just getting by, scared to go outside.

I wish it was easy to ease all pain, for all walks
of life;

too succeed in any way.

Lets not forget, The Justice System failed us
whole;
everything in-between, economically and all.

It could all be different, It all feels opposed;
How did we end up like this? Only in favor of
those.

I believe that death eases all the pain; peace in
heaven and glory,
an aesthetic pleasure, what a beautiful thing to
mourn

When I became a Mother

When I think of the time I became a mother, I
become entirely at peace.
When I watch her smile as she look's at me, I
never felt so completely at ease.
I did not know her two years ago, oh how
unforeseeable life can be.

She stunned me when she came, grasped me to
the life of mothering
I came to perceive what survival really means; I
devoted myself to raise her.
To be the best she can be, to stand by her side
and to love her.

I reclaimed myself and discovered what I had to
offer; I got up,
opened my eyes and looked at the bigger picture.
I am somebody's mother,
my ultimate dream, God knows she means so
much to me.

It restored my sense of belonging; I am more
happy than it may seem.
I found my purpose in living, to show her how
successful I can be.

My biggest success in life, is to watch her watch
me.

I catch sight of myself in her; a beautiful little
girl, pure and gentle, the sweetest in the world.
Dark brown eyes, small circle face, a big burst
of energy that will light up your space.
A personality just like her father, bold and
clever, with the biggest heart ever.

Jane

She sat beside the end table anticipating a new
start of change
Appearing sorrow furthermore timid, staring at
the calendar mid-July
Her checks turning cherry red, eyes watery, she
started to act estrange
She opened the door beside her; there was no
reply

Her name is Jane; she got ready and did her
make-up, to make feel at ease
She wrote herself a love letter, explaining there
is no need to grieve
Turns back a few pages, gasps to find herself on
her knee's
There was a hidden message, she did not know
how to perceive

"Jane, I pray the day you find me; you'll
understand my reasoning then,
take this note to remind you that I love you and
to forgive what I did."
She took a minute to reflect; the handwriting
faded fondly smudged at the end,

No signed signature, her final thought was
uneasy and she stood up to get rid

She took a second look and wonder what it
meant? Who shall write such a deed;
where and when they did? She didn't have an
answer, just done and recede

Duke and Duchess of Sussex

The Royal Wedding at Windsor Castle
In St George's Chapel, filled with warmth of love
Grandson of the Queen; Mr. Prince Harry and
Ms. Meghan Markle

Together as one, they shall rise above
Harmonized in to marriage, with gratitude for the ring
Entitled Duke and Duchess of Sussex, hereby truelove

She is his Queen, and he is her King
May they live with elegance, oh so wholeheartedly
All in honor, hear The Kingdom Choir sing

Complete in happiness, hence so gracefully
Lord bless this family with joy and faithfulness
Archbishop of Canterbury Justin Welby

A beautiful bride walking down in her wedding dress
The Royal Wedding is a stunning thing to witness

16 to 26

Age is just a number,
that's what I've been told.
One day I was 16;
now I'm 26 years old.

I did accomplish lots
but for one thing that I did;
I gave birth and bought life
to a little girl, who gave me
a reason to live

When my girl turns 16,
I'll look back and think.
Where did the time go,
I'll be 41 by then

Time goes by fast,
but we are not there yet.
So I live for these moments,
the time spent with her -
I'll always cherish

Ear muffs

 I asked my daughter for ear muffs; she smiled fondly and gave me hers.

I said "is mine back there?" "You left yours"

That's right, I left them for the little boy to pick up and use.

"What if he doesn't grab them?"

"That's okay sweetie, the next person will."

"Why mom?"

The outside world seems so unkind, I want you to know that kindness still exist.

They maybe just ear muffs, however one needs warm ears too.

After all warm ears equals a good listener and a good listener does their best to help.

"What about cold ears mom?"

Well my girl, cold ears will ache. The ache will cause pain,

the pain will stop you from many things. It won't go away- Until you seek help.

And it's okay to ask for help, never would I want you too not.

You might not realize how your helping others too. "How mom?"

What if that person needed someone to talk to and you came and spoke.

You made them feel valued, just by asking a
simple question starting with hello.
Your voice may be little but it is powerful, don't
you forget.
You come from a family of strong women and
respectful men.
I gave her back her ear muffs; she looked up at
me and said
"Thank you mommy my ears were cold" then
she put it back on her little head.
These are the moments I live for; for teachings
like that.
It's the little things that matter that make it so
worth it.

Broadside

There comes a time to loathe
for what I have to say,
I got nothing to lose, spare or weep.
As an Indigenous Woman,
I sought from surreptitious grounds.
The Indian Act and Numbered Treaties
are just some to mention.
When women go missing,
Its hard to feel safe.
The upbringing of colonization,
downfall's our way of life.
The power we have
is not enough to expose,
All the dirty little secret's
the government holds.

I am her

The little girl in the pink shirt
I am her.
Dancing with her daddy, twirling up high
I am her.
Smiling so big with no front teeth
I am her.
Running to her puppy, no shoes on
I am her.
Runs into adulthood on her own.
I am her.
Takes a few steps back, missing home
I am her.
Finds her way in life day-by-day
I am her.
Creates her own family, long at last
I am her.
Finding her way with her daughter
I am her.
Walks a beautiful path, doesn't look back
I am her.
I am her in this moment.
I love her.

Perspicacious

Perspicacious Woman,
strong and fierce
Observant girl,
loving and pure
She knows what's coming,
she tells her girl
"Follow your dad,
and watch your step
run but don't fall,
I'll be right behind you"
Daddy makes his move,
holding his daughter's hand
Mom takes the haul of
what's not seen in sight of them
In order too succeed
they must not mend,
they stay together,
despite all the criticism

Thrift shop

I took my daughter thrifting,
many stores we went
The one that stood out to her
was the Olive Tree off 50th
We walked inside and looked
there she seen a book stand,
one, two, three, four, five tiny steps
She reached for the big book on top
I've haven't read to her before
She surprises me each day
I grab the pink one for her
She point's and says "yaay"
for only .50 cents,
I've made my daughters day
I can't wait to read this book for her
each and every day

Oatmeal

Oatmeal in the mornings,
cupcakes before bed
Scary movies mid-day,
Lots of convos all night
Coffee for dinner,
Tea for lunch break
Walk for a clear mind,
Jump for happiness
Watch the news on mom's TV,
change the channel to CBC
Take a look outside,
kids running though fall leaves
Smell the muffins cooking,
give your friend a call
Get some fresh air outside
Fuel the days ahead
Never take for granted
What life offers you

Take a nap

During the night we sleep,
mid-day we nap
Nap with the baby,
sleep so soundly.
Dreams of peace,
smile in her sleep
Lovely time to reflect
All the beautiful things
right in front of you
I look to the right,
Who do I see?
A soul so pure
Tiny as can be
At this moment
Is when I feel
my best
and at peace

To the girl that I love most

I love you, I'm proud to be your mom
Your dad loves you immensely
Look at your growth
Your only one years old
May time fly by
as we watch you develop
into your unique self
Ms. Ella-Jane

LOVE

I love early mornings
watching my sweet toddler sleep
I never felt so at peace
When she wakes up
I'll be there
I devoted to never leave her side
Hand by hand
I am here to watch her grow
To make her own decisions
To hear what she has to speak
I'm here to support
No matter what she wants
I'll be her biggest supporter